RACINE'S PHÈDRE

By Jean Racine

(Translated by Harold Anthony Lloyd)

The Characters

Theseus: King of Athens, son of Aegeus.

Phèdre: Present wife of Theseus, daughter of
                    Minos and Pasiphaë, and grand-
                    daughter (through Pasiphaë) of the Sun
                    Helios).

Hippolytus: Son of Theseus and his prior wife
                    Antiope, Queen of the Amazons.

Aricia: Royal Athenian princess.

Oenone: Phèdre's nurse and confidante.

Theramenes: Tutor to Hippolytus.

Ismene: Aricia's confidante.

Panope: A lady in waiting to Phèdre

Guards

The scene is set in Trozene, a Peloponnesian town.

Background

*Theseus, king of Athens, had earlier wed Antiope, Queen of the
Amazons. They had a son, Hippolytus. Theseus subsequently wed
Phèdre, daughter of Minos and a relative of numerous gods through her*

grandfather, the Sun (Helios). Phèdre then fell in love with Hippolytus. To disguise her feelings, she had Hippolytus exiled. The play begins with Hippolytus abroad in Trozene.

Translator's Note: To accommodate the different rhythm of English, I have generally rendered the French alexandrine couplets into iambic pentameter ones. To accommodate further the linguistic difference, I have freely used enjambment. I agree with Richard Wilbur that stacking up end-stopped lines in English can sound like piling lumber.

ACT I

Scene 1

(Hippolytus, Theramenes)

Hippolytus

Dear Theramenes, I've made up my mind
To end my stay in Trozene[1] now. I find
Myself consumed here with the gravest doubt
About myself. I blush in shame about
My sloth. Six months my Father's[2] been away
And yet Hippolytus can't even say
He knows his hiding place or that he's well.

Theramenes

But where, Sir, would you seek him now? Please tell
Me. Where I knew to look I've also tried
To find him. I've crossed both seas[3] that divide
Great Corinth, and I've heard what people said
Where Acheron[4] is lost among the dead.
I've tried Tenaros[5] and Elidos, too,

---

[1] A city in Greece on the Peloponnesus.

[2] His father is Theseus, son of Aegeus who was the king of Athens.

[3] The Ionian and Aegean Seas.

[4] An underworld river sometimes considered the boundary of Hades
over which dead souls were ferried into the underworld.

4

And even crossed the sea[6] where Icarus flew.
By what new hope and in what other place
Could you succeed instead to find some trace
Of Theseus? Who knows--perhaps he's tried
To keep his place a secret and to hide.
Perhaps while we are fearing for him so
He covers up a love we shouldn't know
And simply waits until some woman can....

Hippolytus

Stop, Theramenes, and respect the man
Who's long outgrown his youthful errors. He
Is not detained that way. We all can see
That Phèdre's[7] stopped a heart that used to roam
And long has feared no rivals in her home.
No, I must find him. I must sail away
From here and search. I dare no longer stay.

Theramenes

Since when, my Lord, were you so fast to sail
From peaceful lands your childhood loved so well,
From lands I've often seen were your resort
From all the pomp and tumult of the Court?

---

[5] Now Cape Matapan on the Greek mainland.

[6] The Sea around Icaria, the island where Icarus washed ashore.

[7] Wife of Theseus, step-mother of Hippolytus, and daughter of Minos,
King of Crete and Pasiphae who was the daughter of Helios and Circe's
sister Perseis.

What danger or what sadness drives you so?

Hippolytus

The happy times are gone. All changed to woe
Now that the gods have sent us by the Sea
That Queen from Minos and Pasiphaë.[8]

Theramenes

I understand your sadness all too well.
You think of Phèdre and your thoughts still dwell
On your stepmother's hatred, her demand
That you be exiled to some foreign land.
And yet those hatreds that she had for you
Have gone--at least relaxed. Consider, too,
Why should you have such endless fears and run
From one who's dying, wishing it were done?
She's sick with some strange illness but won't tell
The cause. She's tired of light and life as well.
In such a state how could she scheme or plot?

Hippolytus

Her vain hostility? I fear it not.
I'm leaving to avoid another foe:
Admittedly Aricia's why I go,
Whose family long conspired against my own.

---

[8] I.e., Phèdre.

Theramenes

Her persecution, too, you would condone
When you well know this sister Pallantid[9]
Has never joined in what her brothers did?
How can you hate an innocent like her?

Hippolytus

If I despised her, I would stay. Be sure.

Theramenes

May I attempt an explanation? Could
You now no longer be the Prince who would
For ever be the enemy of Love
He often saw his King the victim of?
Could Venus scorned so long by all your pride
At last show Theseus was justified?
By making you like other men as well,
You worship at her altars now? Pray tell,
Sir, could you be in love?

Hippolytus

How dare you say!

---

[9] Children of Pallas who stole Athens from his brother Aegeus. Theseus
killed Pallas and his fifty giant sons.

You've known my heart and its unwavering way
From my own birth and yet would question now
If I have strayed? I never break a vow!
Nursed by a mother Amazon[10] I must
Have confidence and strength. And you can trust
I've only strengthened with the passing years
With traits my father gave. For it appears
My mettle parallels your tales to me
Of great things in my father's history.
You know how much my heart craved every word
Of every noble exploit that I heard
When you portrayed a hero brave and deft
Consoling men when Hercules had left,
Who strangled monsters, gave thieves punishment,
Like Sinnis, Scirron, Cercyon[11] he rent
In Epidaurus flinging bones in scores
While Crete smoked with the blood of Minotaurs--
And yet you told of base things at his hands,
Like promises he broke in many lands,
Or Helen stolen by his trickery,
Or awful tears[12] he made Salamis[13] see,
And many others, names that he forgot,
Too willing to believe love they should not--
Like Ariadne stranded[14] once he's through,

---

[10] The mother of Hippolytus was the Amazon Antiope. Antiope was
sister of the Amazonian Queen Hippolyta.
[11] Racine also inserts Procrustes (who cut or stretched travellers to
make them fit his bed) which I omit for meter's sake. The others
referenced are also various monsters or robbers.
[12] The tears of Periboea one of the girls Theseus had abandoned.
[13] An island off Attica's coast.

8

And Phèdre (though on better terms) seized, too--
You know I hated every dark report.
I begged and pleaded that you cut those short
Wishing I could crush and throw away
Every evil deed I heard you say--
Shall I in turn be bound in slavery next?
Would the gods have me so humbled, vexed
When my weak will would be more guilty where
It lacks the many honors that would spare
A Theseus? I've killed no monsters, none
That give me leave to fail as he has done.
And if my pride dried up, still after all
Could I pick Aricia for my fall?
Would I not still remember that we are
Eternally divided, split afar?
My father disapproves. His law's severe
Forbidding nephews for her brothers here
That would revive their clan. With her made chaste,
The sister can assure the name's erased.
With Aricia under such law banned
From marriage, I can never have her hand.
Should I defend her rights against his rage?
Is that a foolish battle I should wage
And set out on a course of reckless love....

Theramenes

But if the gods ordain it from above

---

[14] Daughter of the King of Crete whom Theseus abandoned on Naxos after she had helped him escape from the Minotaur

9

It hardly matters what he might forbid.
It makes her more appealing. What he did
Is stoke your passion and make you rebel
And find attractive what he would repel.
Why should you fear a love so dignified?
Why shouldn't something sweet as that be tried?
Why must you trust in timid scruples? Do
You fear you'll stray down Hercules' path, too?
What fortitude has Venus not subdued?
Where would you be (who fight this constant feud
With her) if your mother had done the same
And put a damper on a father's flame?
What good are all these things that you avow?
Confess it. All is change. It's quite clear now
We hardly see the proud and savage way
You rode your chariot just yesterday
About the shore in practice of the skill
That Neptune first invented. Standing still,
It's clear we echo in the forests less
And your long eyes have secrets they confess.
I cannot doubt you love. I see you burn
And perish from the thing you claim to spurn.
Are you not pleased by all her charms you've seen?

Hippolytus

I'm off to find my father, Theramene.

Theramenes

Won't you see Phèdre first before you go?

10

Hippolytus

I planned to do so.   You may tell her so.
I'm duty bound and cannot tell her though--
But what new trouble grieves Oenone so?

Scene 2

(Hippolytus, Oenone, Theramenes)

Oenone

Alas, my lord, whose troubles are as great
As mine? The Queen dies. We've not long to wait.
In vain I've watched her night and day while she
Sinks in my arms of ills she hides from me.
An endless chaos overtakes her head.
An awful sadness drags her from her bed.
Her profound sadness (even in the day)
Requires I order all her guests away---
She's coming.

Hippolytus

That's enough. I'll leave her so
I don't display a face that brings more woe.

Scene 3

(Phèdre, Oenone)

Phèdre

Let's stay here, go no further, Oenone.
I can't bear up. My strength's abandoned me.
My eyes are dazzled by the daylight and
My trembling knees give way. I cannot stand.
Alas!

(She sits)

Oenone

Oh gods! May tears relieve her ails!

Phèdre

How vain these jewels! How heavy are these veils!
And what obtrusive person took the care
To tie up all these knots within my hair?
How everything conspires affliction, wrong!

Oenone

Your wishes clash! This can't go on for long!
You are condemning now the very way
You ordered we adorn you here today

When you had roused your past strengths so you might
Display yourself again and see the light--
And yet as soon as you see any day
You hate it fast and wish to hide away.

Phèdre

O Sun[15], of which my mother boasted kin,
Perhaps you blush as I last take you in.

Oenone

What? Won't you leave that cruel urge behind?
You always give up life? Am I to find
You always planning for the day you're dead?

Phèdre

I'd rather sit in shady woods instead--
There I can see that solar chariot fly
Around its dusty course before my eye.

Oenone

What?

---

[15] Pheadra has Solar descent through her mother Pasiphae, daughter of Helios.

Phèdre

Am I mad? Where now? What did I say?
I think my mind was wandering astray--
It's hardly usable. The gods instead
Have stolen it! My face is now all red!
I've let you see my shameful sorrows here
Too much. Unwillingly, my eyes now tear.

Oenone

If you must blush, let silence make you red
For all the harm it does your heart and head.
Rejecting all our care, deaf to each word,
How could your death wish still be undeterred?
What fury cuts your life span such a way?
What charm or poison dries its source away?
The shadows have three times obscured the skies
Since any sleep has come upon your eyes
And day has three times chased away the night
Since you've allowed your mouth a single bite.
What frightful scheme have you allowed to tempt
You so? What justifies what you attempt?
Would you offend the gods who gave you life?
Would you betray the vows you took as wife?
Would you betray at last your children whom
You would condemn to servitude, to doom?
Know that such awful deeds would also don
The crown upon that half-bred Amazon,
That haughty hater of you and your kin,
Hippolytus whose first days were within

That brutish woman....

Phèdre

Gods!

Oenone

That troubled you.

Phèdre

Who's that again, unhappy woman? Who?

Oenone

Ha! Reason grants you anger without blame.
I joy to see you shake at his foul name.
Yes, live. Let love and duty make you brave.
Choose life. Don't let some Scythian's son enslave
And crush your children who are better bred
From gods[16] and from the best of Greece instead.
Agree with me. Each moment kills you more.
You must be quick. It's time must you restore
Your failing energies, your smoldering fire
Before the torch's flickers last expire.

---

[16] I.e., they are descended from the Sun through Phèdre and her mother.

15

Phèdre

I've drawn my guilty life out much too long.

Oenone

What deep remorse could tear your heart? What wrong
Could you have done that troubles you this way?
Your hands aren't stained with guiltless blood are they?

Phèdre

Thank Heaven both my hands are clean. I would
But beg the gods my heart were just as good!

Oenone

What frightening scheme have you conceived that may
Now terrify your heart in such a way?

Phèdre

I've said enough. Please spare me from the rest.
I die to keep such horror unconfessed.[17]

---

[17] The psychological depths of Phèdre are of course profound as will
become more and more apparent as the play progresses. Here Phèdre
engages in the most basic self-defense mechanism: repression.

Oenone

Then die with your mean secrecy in tact
But find another hand to do the act.
As long as life remains in you, I would
Die first and go to Hell before you could.
A thousand open roads forever run
Below and I would choose the shortest one.
Mean woman, have I ever lied to you?
Don't you remember I helped birth you, too?
For you I left my country, children yet
This is the only gratitude I get?

Phèdre

What can you hope to gain by pressing me?
You'll shake with horror if I grant your plea.

Oenone

What could you tell me that could terrify
Me more than watching my poor Phèdre die?

Phèdre

But if you were to hear my fate and crime,
I'd die no less—just shamed more at the time.

Oenone

Please, Madam, in the name of every tear
I've shed for you, your knees I'm grasping here,
Please tell me what this matter is about.

Phèdre

You asked for it. Stand up.

Oenone

I hear. Speak out.

Phèdre

Gods! What am I to say? Where shall I start?

Oenone

Such foolish fears--stop tearing me apart.

Phèdre

Oh, ire of Venus setting all askew
Including errors it made Mother do!

Oenone

Forget them, Madam. Let the moment cast
Them far back in the long forgotten past.

Phèdre

My sister, Ariadne, wounded by
What love? What left her there alone to die?!

Oenone

What's this? What awful cares make you begin
Today attacking all your closest kin?

Phèdre

Since Venus wants it so[18] I'll perish worst
Of all my awful family. I'm cursed.

Oenone

Are you in love?

---

[18] Phèdre knows she has not chosen the love she alludes to. (Is it even possible to do so in the ordinary sense of the terms?) As she has done nothing voluntarily here, how can she be guilty of any sin? Racine's Jansenism would hold her out as an example of man's inherently evil nature which can only be saved by Grace. Yet, of course, this would seem to beg the original question of how one can be blamed for something one did not voluntarily choose.

Phèdre

Consumed with all its rage.

Oenone

With whom?

Phèdre

I'll speak the horrible outrage--
His name....It makes me tremble, shudder so.
I love....

Oenone

Who then?

Phèdre

It's someone that you know--
That Amazonian prince I've long oppressed.

Oenone

Hippolytus? Great gods!

Phèdre

As you attest!

Oenone

Oh me! My blood has frozen in the vein.
What crime, despair, what wretched family's pain!
What awful voyage! Why has Fate forced us
To land on shores so vile and dangerous?

Phèdre

My ills go further back. Just married to
Aegeus' son my peace and fortune, too,
Seemed all assured. Then Athens showed to me
The man who turned my haughty enemy.
I saw him, blushed and then grew pale. My heart
Was all bewildered from the very start.
My eyes no longer saw. I lost my voice.
I felt my body freeze and burn at once.
I knew that Venus stalks us with her flame
To sear our family more. I knew her aim.
My constant prayers I thought would turn her round.
I built a temple, fancied up its ground.
Then always in my sacrifices I
Investigated entrails seeking why
My reason strayed. Weak cures for fatal love!
In vain I burned incense for her above--
For though my mouth implored her name I still

Adored Hippolytus,[19] his sight a thrill,
There even at the altars where I came
To offer all to a god I dared not name.[20]
I tried avoiding him in every place
And yet I'd see him in his father's face!
At last I turned against my being and
Tried persecuting him with my own hand--
To drive this foe I loved away from me
I feigned I had a new wife's jealousy.
I sought exile, his banishment I pressed
Till I had torn him from his father's breast.
Oenone, I could breathe. With him way
My conscience was in much less disarray.
My troubles hidden, yielding to my spouse,
I raised the offspring of our fatal house.
What useless caution! As cruel fate had planned,
My husband brought me here to Trozene and
I faced again the person I had banned!
At once my fresh wound bled. It could not stand
The sight again of such sweet contraband.
I'm prey that Venus clutches in her hand![21]
Though forced to love, I've proper hatred for
My crime. My life and passion I abhor--

---

[19] Not only has Phèdre not chosen this unlawful love, she has in fact
worked hard to choose the opposite without success. This would seem
to make the question of moral culpability here even more difficult.
[20] Compare Racine's "ce dieu que je n'osais nommer" with Lord Alfred
Douglas's "I am the Love that dare not speak its name."
[21] Although rhyme in succeeding couplets can be accidental or of no
import, the rhyme in these *three* couplets does not seem accidental but
seems to underscore Phèdre's dementia.

By dying I would have my glory back
And keep the light of day off love so black.
Yet I could not withstand your tears, your force,
And spoke. I've no regret although, of course,
I need assurance you won't interfere
Or give reproach now that my death is near,
That you will cease your vain attempts to save
A dying sinner ready for her grave.

Scene 4

(Phèdre, Oenone, Panope)

Panope

I'd rather hide this sad news from you; yet,
I must reveal it. Madame, I regret
Your husband's dead. The strong man lost his life.
The last to hear the bad news is his wife.

Oenone

What did you say, Panope?

Panope

                                    That the Queen
Would ask in vain for gods to intervene
And bring back Theseus. New ships in port
Just gave Hippolytus the sad report.

Phèdre

Oh Heavens!

Panope

Athens can't agree upon
Her king. Half of the city now supports your son.
The rest would crown (in breach of Athens' law)
An alien's son instead of yours. We saw
Some others even scheming round a plan
That would enthrone Aricia and her clan.
I felt I had to warn you. We believe
Hippolytus is even set to leave
And in this present storm should he appear
The fickle crowd would follow him we fear.

Oenone

Panope, that's enough. The Queen has heard
You well and will react to every word.

Scene 5

(Phèdre, Oenone)

Oenone

I'd ceased my pleas for you to live and I
Had planned to join you in the grave and die.

24

I'd lost my heart to stop what you had planned.
But this new evil makes a new demand.
Your fortune's changed, has donned another face.
The King is gone and you must take his place.
He leaves a son and you have duties now
To live and make him king. You can't allow
His bondage with your death. For then who would
Assist him, wipe his tears as mothers should?
No, live and live beyond reproach. For now
Your love is ordinary. Laws allow
It. Theseus in dying broke the knot
That stitched your awful problems. You should not
Now fear Hippolytus, of course, because
Your loving him no longer breaks the laws.
And yet perhaps in fearing you he's said
He'll lead the rebels, serve them as their head.
Correct his error, bend his courage and
Dissuade the lucky man. Trozene's his land.
But he knows well the law will give your son
The grand ramparts Minerva built.[22] Be one
In taking on a common enemy,
And thereby seek a common victory.

Phèdre

All right! I'll let your counsel rescue me.
I'll live if life's a possibility,
If mother love can reinvigorate
A failing heart in such a weakened state.

---

[22] I.e., Athens.

ACT II

Scene 1

(Aricia, Ismene)

Aricia

Hippolytus has asked to see me now?
He comes to tell me he is leaving? How
Can you be sure, Ismene, that is true?

Ismene

Because of the King's death—that means that you
Must steel yourself and be prepared to see
The many who will woo you now your're free.
At last you are the mistress of your fate,
And all of Greece will soon be at your feet.

Aricia

Is that not baseless rumor? What now frees
Me from so many of my enemies?

Ismene

The gods no more oppose you, Madame, now

The King has joined your brothers down below.

Aricia

What final feat has killed him? Have you heard?

Ismene

There are so many tales of what occurred.
Some say that having seized another girl
The waves engulfed the cheater in a swirl.
While others say--this rumor's everywhere--
He went to Hell with Pirithoüs[23] where
He saw the dark Cocytus[24] and displayed
His flesh. His arrogance was unafraid.
Despite such bluster, he soon came to learn
The nature of that place of no return.

Aricia

Could I believe some mortal not yet dead
Could tunnel down to Hell as you said?
What charm in that grim place could make him go?

Ismene

He's dead and you alone would doubt it so.

---

[23] According to Racine, this journey was made to visit a king whose wife
Pirithoüs wished to steal.
[24] An underworld river.

Now Athens groans and Trozene knows it's true
And sees Hippolytus as king now, too.
Within the palace, trembling for her son,
Now Phèdre seeks advice from everyone.

Aricia

But do you think Hippolytus could be
Less vicious than his father was to me?
Or pity my misfortunes now?

Ismene

I do.

Aricia

Does he not seem unfeeling, though, to you?
How could you think he'd show respect to me
When he disdains all women equally?
He shuns our steps. He is fastidious
In keeping refuge far away from us.

Ismene

I know the frigid stories people tell
And yet I've seen him near you, child, as well.
Such fabled pride was one I had to see--
It doubled up my curiosity.
I studied him and found him not so grim.
Your first encounter much affected him.

28

He vainly tried to turn away his eyes
But weakness made him do quite otherwise.
He may not like the name of lover; yet,
His plaintive eyes betray his frigid mouth.

Aricie

Although there's little proof supporting you,
My heart of course imagines it were true.
And yet could one who knows me well believe
That such a toy of Fate could now have leave
Of constant bitterness and tears, could know
Such love? I am alone in all my woe.
The last blood of my line is left in me,
The sole survivor of war's cruelty.
In the flower of youth, I now have lost
Six brothers of a noble house so crossed.
The sword hacked them until the ground was red
As Erectheus'[25] nephews lay and bled.
You know that since their death the law's severe.
No Greek may have good feelings for me. Fear
Makes law--a sister's reckless passion might
Just make her brothers' cinders reignite!
But then you knew I was not amorous.
I often thanked old, unjust Theseus
Whose rigors merely seconded my scorn--
I had not seen his son some said was born.
We met and there was some surrender--I

---

[25] Earth's son, raised by Athena. He was a king of Athens and an ancestor of both Theseus and of Pallas.

Admired such grace and bloom before my eye.
Sweet Nature gave such gifts to him and yet
He hates her bounty. He lives to forget
He has them. Love? I find there nobleness,
His father's good without his sinfulness.
I love, I will admit, his noble pride
That never let the yoke of love be tied
Round him. Phèdre is little honored by
That liberal love of Theseus. No, I
Am much too proud to share love offered to
A thousand whores and tramps to sample, too.
I'd rather bend some bendless bravery
And bring some sadness to stolidity
And bind a slave surprised to see a chain
That yokes so tight that fighting is in vain.
That's my desire instead. Great Hercules
Was conquered and disarmed with greater ease
So all his conquerors could never be
Entitled to the laurels due to me
Should I prevail!   And yet, how silly I'd
Be having hope. All others failed who tried.
Perhaps you soon will hear me sadly say
I'm injured by the pride I praise today.
Hippolytus could love? How could I be
So fortunate....

Ismene

You'll hear it now. For he
Is coming.

Scene 2

(Hippolytus, Aricia, Ismene)

Hippolytus

Madame, just before I go
I thought your changing fate you now should know.
My father's dead. My doubts were proper. They
Suspected why he stayed so long away--
Death alone could shackle one so strong
And hide him from the Universe so long.
The gods at last permitted death to seize
This friend, successor, mate of Hercules.
I think your hate will spare his virtues and
Allow the praise such heroes must command
While one hope soothes the mortal grief in me:
Your guardian's gone and I can set you free.
I now revoke the laws restraining you
And free you as your heart would have you do.
I'm now the king with means to do it. Ma'am
I set you free, much freer than I am.

Aricia

Please curb your kindness. I'm embarrassed by
The excess. Sir, such care to honor my
Disgrace just binds me more than you could know

31

Beneath the laws that you would overthrow.

Hippolytus

It seems that Athens is uncertain who
Should claim the crown. The queen's son? I? Or you[26]?

Aricia

You said my name?

Hippolytus

             Their laws could be too proud
To recognize my claim. The Greeks are loud
In censure of my foreign mother. Yet
My half-brother alone makes no real threat
Since I have rights prevailing over him
The law must recognize however prim.
I'm held back by a much more proper brake.
I cede, no, recognize that you should take
The ancient scepter your ancestors raised
Through that world-conquering mortal so long praised[27].
Adoption put it in Aegeus' hand.
And Athens benefited so the land
Was glad to recognize a generous throne
And cast your brothers off as they have done.

---

[26] As noted above, the descendants of Pallas also claim the throne of
Athens.

[27] Presumably Erectheus.

Today the City calls you back to quell
Disputes now suffered much too long. None will
Now stain this ground with more blood from a race
That sprang in ancient times from just this place.
Trozene obeys me and the fields of Crete
Would offer Phèdre's son a good retreat.
All Attica is yours. By leaving, you
Can unify what we would break in two.

Aricia

Astonished and confused by all I hear,
I have some fear I must be dreaming here.
Am I awake? Could such a plan be true?
What god has planted all of this in you?
I have long known your glory is widespread.
Yet how much greater is the truth instead!
You would betray yourself to favor me?
Was not your lack of hate, hostility
Enough? Or that your own soul never grew
Its animosity....

Hippolytus

What? I hate you?
What savage manners and what hardened hate
Could the sweet sight of you not mitigate?
Could such deceptive charms be challenged here....

Aricia

What?

Hippolytus

I have said too much too soon I fear.
I see that reason gives away to force.
Since I've begun to talk, I'll stay the course.
This prince who proudly fought off love's rule and
So long insulted those in her command,
Who also mocked the feeble mortals who
Wrecked in her storms (as he would never do)
Now finds her laws enslaving him as well.
Her storms now drag him howling in their swell.
One moment conquered my audacity
And substituted new dependency.
For six months, I've been desperate and ashamed.
My flesh still bears the many darts love aimed
At me. I've fought against us both in vain.
So now I flee. Though absent, you'll remain
With me. Always your image will pursue
Me, and the light of day--the darkness, too--
Will always show your charms. I try to flee
But know the world has made a slave of me.
Despite the pains and cares I took before
I look for me but find myself no more.
My javelin, bow and chariot do no good
With Neptune's arts no longer understood.
My lonely groans bounce in the woods. I've found

My idle nags don't recognize the sound.
Perhaps my talk of such wild love you bring
Me, makes you blush in hearing such a thing?
What savage means to offer love to you!
How strange the captive who is fettered, too!
But that should make the offer much more dear.
Pretend I speak a foreign language here
And don't reject my offer just because
The rhetoric is bad — you are the cause.

Scene 3

(Hippolytus, Aricia, Theramenes, Ismene)

Theramenes

The Queen is coming, Sir, whom I precede.
She looks for you.

Hippolytus

For me?

Theramenes

                Yes, Sir. Indeed,
She's sent me here for reasons I don't know
To say she'd like to speak before you go.

Hippolytus

The Queen? What could I tell her? What could she....

Aricia

If she would speak you cannot disagree.
However certain of her hatred, you
Must still allow some pity for her, too.

Hippolytus

And yet you go and leave me as before--
I'll wonder if I've hurt one I adore.
I'll wonder if my heart left in your hand....

Aricia

Go, Prince, and do what you have kindly planned
And give me Athens. I will gratefully
Accept all gifts you wish to give to me.
Yet this grand empire that I now shall take
From you is not the dearest gift you make.

Scene 4

(Hippolytus, Theramenes)

Hippolytus

Are we now ready, friend? But there's the Queen.

Please go assure that nothing's unforeseen
In our departure. Give the orders fast
Then call me so this interview can't last.

Scene 5

(Phèdre, Hippolytus, Oenone)

Phèdre

He's here and all my blood runs to my heart.
His sight makes me forget where I should start.

Oenone

Think of a son whose only hope is you.

Phèdre

They say you plan a prompt departure to
Some far-off place. I've come to add my tears
To your misfortune and to state my fears
For my son who has lost his father and
Will see his mother's death soon. Thousands stand
Already to attack his childhood. You
Alone can stop the awful things they'd do.
And yet a secret sadness troubles me.
I fear I've made you deaf to his poor plea.

I fear your righteous anger sees the son
As means to punish what a mother's done.

Hippolytus

I'd never think of anything so low.

Phèdre

I'd not complain if you despise me so.
You saw how I have tried to harm you. Still,
You could not read my heart. It was goodwill
In fact to cause your hatred of me. I
Was deeply troubled when you were close by
Me. Publicly and privately I said
I wished that seas divided us instead.
I even made a law specifically
Forbidding mention of your name to me.
But if we measure penalty to crime,
If only ill will draws your hatred, I'm
Then most deserving of your sympathy
And least deserving of antipathy.

Hippolytus

A second wife won't have her child outdone.
She's rarely kind to any other's son.
Suspicions like you have are common where
Your role as wife is one you've had to share.
All other women would have done it, too,
And might have made me suffer more than you.

38

Phèdre

Ah, Sir--I dare to say it--Heaven's made
Me an exception to that. I'm afraid
Another trouble eats me to the core.

Hippolytus

You have no need to worry any more.
Perhaps your husband lives and you will learn
He has the gods' permission to return.
Neptune protects him. He will not remain
Unmoved and let my father plead in vain.

Phèdre

One never sees death's shore two times. Since he
Has seen that gloomy beach, no hope could be
For any god to send him back some day.
The stingy Acheron won't free its prey.
What did I say? He lives. He breathes in you.
I see my husband in your eyes. I do.
I see and talk to him. My soul.... I stray.
In spite of me, my mad heart has its say.

Hippolytus

I see the great effects of your love. I
Know, though he's dead, he seems before your eye.
Your love of him stays always in your heart.

Phèdre

I long for him. It's tearing me apart.
I love him not as he is now in Hell,
The flighty flirt of thousands who as well
Now brings dishonor to that final bed.
It's faithful, proud, brave Theseus instead
Who carried youth and charm as gods would do
That I would love--those things I see in you.
He had your walk, your eyes, your voice and he
Could blush with your same noble modesty
While sailing through the waves into our Crete
When he was one all local girls would meet.
What were you doing then, Hippolytus,
When he assembled his elite for us?
Perhaps you were too young to join them and
Make such a passage with them to our land?
You would have killed the Cretan monster[28] though
He had that endless maze that served him so.
And helping you to navigate instead
My sister would have handed you the thread[29]--
But no, in this dream I would come before
Her. Love would make me do that. Furthermore,
I'd be the one who helped you learn the way
To navigate the maze and get away.
How much I would have cared for your sweet head!
I'd not be satisfied with but a thread!

---

[28] Again, the Minotaur.
[29] I.e., Ariadne would have given him (instead of Theseus) the ball of
thread to use to escape from the maze.

I would have shared the danger with you, too.
I surely would have walked ahead of you.
I would have joined you in the maze so I
Could join in the endeavor live or die.

Hippolytus

Good gods! What do I hear? Do you forget
That he's my father and your husband yet?

Phèdre

Forget his memory? What could make you say
That? Could I ever act in such a way?

Hippolytus

Oh, please forgive me, Madame. I admit
The wrong in my accusing you of it.
I'm so ashamed I cannot look at you.
I'll leave....

Phèdre

Ah, harsh one! You[30] have heard me too
Well. I have said enough so there can be

---

[30] In the French, the shocking nature of this is underscored as Phèdre
slips at this point into the familiar "tu" form of address.

No room to err. You know the love in me
For you. Yet do not think despite the sight
Of your innocence, I still think I am right.
Don't think the crazy love consuming me
Could be a poison I took willingly.[31]
Unlucky pawn of heaven's vengeance, I
Detest me more than you could ever try.
The gods themselves would testify that they
Have made my body burn in such a way,
Those gods who glorify their cruel art
Of playing with a feeble human heart.
And even you must still recall it, too.
I hardly kept away. I hounded you.
Inhuman, awful, any such pretense--
I'd hate instead of love you in defense.[32]
And yet what good did all my efforts do?
You hate me more. I've no less love for you.
I found your increased trouble just endears.
I've languished, withered, burned, and stayed in tears.
You only need to use your eyes to see
I speak the truth if you can look at me.
What do I say? You don't think I confess
Such shame without compulsion? I address
You trembling so I don't betray my son
And ask that you not hate that little one.
Oh what a project for a person who

---

[31] Again, Phèdre has plainly not chosen how she loves.
[32] Phèdre's complex psychological development continues. Here she admits the common self-defense mechanism of reaction formation: she has tried to prevent a dangerous desire by actively endorsing its opposite.

Is so in love she only talks of you!
Have vengeance! Scourge my awful love and me!
You noble hero's son act forcefully!
The widow loves the son! What could be worse!
Remove that evil from the universe!
That frightful beast is something you must slay.
Here is my heart and strike it now I say.
I am impatient to expunge the sin
And feel the blows before your hands begin.
Strike now! Or would that be too low for you?
Do you begrudge me my correction, too?
Or do you think vile blood would stain your hand?
Then strike me with your sword right where I stand.
Kill me!

Oenone

Why are you acting as you do?
But someone comes. Let's have no witness. To
Avoid the shame, please leave now hastily.

Scene 6

(Hippolytus, Theramenes)

Theramenes

That's Phèdre rushing, dragged along I see?
Why do you seem so sad, Sir? Why do I
Now see you without sword or color? Why?

43

Hippolytus

Let's run from here. I've had the worst surprise.
I'm terrified to look in my own eyes.
Phèdre...no--my silence I shall keep.
This awful secret must be buried deep.

Theramenes

The sail is ready if you wish to go.
But Athens made a choice. It's time you know.
Your brother won the vote throughout the land.
It seems that Phèdre has the upper hand.

Hippolytus

Phèdre?

Theramenes

A herald just arrived to say
It's Athens' will. The throne has passed today.
Her son's the king.

Hippolytus

You gods who know her, how
Could justice sanction such injustice now?

Theramenes

And yet some rumors say that Theseus
Is still alive and seen in Epirus.[33]
But I who searched that place for him know he....

Hippolytus

No matter. We'll observe all thoroughly.
This rumor must be traced back to its source,
And if there's nothing there to change our course,
We'll sail. No matter what the cost may be,
The scepter must be held in dignity.

---

[33] An ancient realm on the Ionian Sea in modern North-West Greece
and Southern Albania.

ACT III

Scene 1

(Phèdre, Oenone)

Phèdre

Ah! They should take these honors elsewhere. You
Would irk me now? You wish they saw me, too?
How would you help my devastated mind?
I've talked too much. Hide me where none can find.
It spreads abroad--or so my anger's dared.
I've spoken things that never should be aired.
Oh, heavens, how unfeeling was the way
He listened and avoided what I'd say!
His only thought was how fast he could flee
While all his blushing heaped more shame on me!
Why did you try to thwart my death request?
And when his sword was searching for my breast,
He turned quite pale and tried to pull it back
Too late before I touched it. It is black
With my contamination now, and therefore he
Will always see it as profanity[34].

---

[34] Phèdre's psychological defense mechanisms also include fantasy: she is obviously fantasizing about an inanimate object in a sexual way.

Oenone

Would it not be much better if you sought
Some higher care as Minos' daughter ought?
Reject an ingrate who would run away
And rule a state that's willing to obey.

Phèdre

I rule?! How govern any polity
When my weak reason cannot govern me?
When I have lost dominion of my sense?
When choked with shame and all its consequence?
When I am dying?

Oenone

Run.

Phèdre

I must stay. He....

Oenone

You can't leave one you've banished recently?

Phèdre

That time has passed. He knows my madness. He
Knows I have crossed all bounds of decency.
I told my victor all my shame, my ill.
Hope slid into my heart against my will.
Yet it was you who wouldn't let me die,
Who stopped my soul already on the fly
Just at my lips. You flattered me and brought
Me back. I might still love or so you thought.

Oenone

What good or guilty thing could I not do
To save you from whatever's plaguing you?
But if his earlier actions caused offense
How can you now ignore the man's pretense?
Or how his harsh eyes watched you prostrate there
Before him as he left you in despair?
His savage pride has made him awful! Why
Can Phèdre not see this as well as I?

Phèdre

He could shake off this pride that bothers you.
Raised in the woods, he's learned its roughness, too.
Made hard by savage laws, Hippolytus
Has never heard the love he heard from us--
Perhaps his silence came from his surprise

And our complaints were too strong otherwise.[35]

Oenone

But don't forget the savage mother of.....

Phèdre

Though Scythian and savage, she could love.

Oenone

He has a fatal hatred for our sex.

Phèdre

Then I will have no rivals who could vex
My plans. Your counsel is late anyhow--
Please help my passion, not my reason now.
Since he can wall out love with his hard heart
We'll have to find some less-defended part.
An empire's charms appeared to move him. He
Could not hide Athens' pull on him. We see
His ships already pointed there, each sail
Abandoned to the first winds that prevail.
Go find that young ambitious man for me.

---

[35]Racine continues to build Phèdre's complex psychological profile.
Phèdre now employs the common self defense mechanisms of denial
(i.e., refusing to see the likely meaning of Hippolytus's actions) and
rationalization (i.e., trying to prove that she is acting reasonably here
and her actions should therefore be approved).

Display the glittering crown for him to see
A sacred diadem for his young brow.
I want the honor to bestow it now.
The power I cannot keep, let's give away
To one who'll teach my son the proper way
To rule. Perhaps he'll take the father's role
With son and mother both in his control.
Try every means to win him over. He
Is more receptive to you than to me.
Wail "Phèdre's dying." Cry and grasp in need.
Don't be too shy to supplicate and plead.
I've told you all. My hope is just in you.
I'll learn from your return what I must do.

Scene 2

(Phèdre alone)

Phèdre

O Venus, you have seen my fall, my shame.
Am I not crushed enough? Or would you maim
Me further? Do you lack the will to quit?
Your triumph's perfect. All your arrows hit.
Harsh goddess, if you want a victory
Attack a man who's more your enemy.
Hippolytus avoids you. He will not
Kneel at your altars. He's a bigger blot
On you. He seems offended by your name.
Avenge yourself--our interest is the same.
Just let him love....I hear Oeone's walk.

Oenone? He hates me and would not talk....

Scene 3

(Phèdre, Oenone)

Oenone

You must now change your focus of despair.
Lost virtue now must be your only care.
For I have learned that Theseus is here--
The King we once thought dead will soon appear!
The people run and rush to see him. When
I sought Hippolytus (as you, my Queen,
Had ordered), I could hear their shouts round me....

Phèdre

My husband lives. Enough said, Oenone.
I spoke of love my husband will abhor.
He lives. I'd rather not know any more.

Oenone

What?

Phèdre

        I predicted this but your tears pled
With me until I did the things you said.
I would have died with dignity that morn.

Instead by your advice I'll die in scorn.[36]

Oenone

You'll die?

Phèdre

Good heavens! What have I now done?
My husband comes and he will bring his son!
The very witness of that evil thing
Will watch to see if I dare greet the King
While my heart breaks of love Hippolytus
Ungratefully considers scandalous.
And yet perhaps in honor of the King
He might conceal it, never say a thing?
Could he subject his King and father to
Such treason? Is that something he could do?
Yet either way it matters not. I, too,
Know what I did. I'm not the woman who
Can calmly taste the fruits of felony
Yet never blush at all or seem carefree.
I know my passions. I recall them all.
It seems these vaults as well as every wall
Conceal a mouth preparing to proclaim
To Theseus my actions and my shame.
The time has come to end my life so I
Am saved by death.[37] Is it so bad to die?

---

[36] Phèdre now engages in the common psychological defense
mechanism of projection: she projects the cause of her troubles on
Oenone. Yet, if Oenone's advice was bad, why did she take it?

52

Death brings no fear to sadness of my kind.
I only fear the name I'll leave behind.
I leave my children my sad legacy.
Yet blood from Jupiter[38] brings bravery
As they should find--but even blood so strong
Must feel the weight of their own mother's wrong.
I tremble that some words said truthfully
Will cause them all reproach because of me
And that such weight will soon immobilize
Them till they dare not gaze in others' eyes.

Oenone

I have to pity them and I agree
Your fear is justified as fear can be.
But why should you subject them to the shame
That comes from your admitting any blame?
They'll say that guilt was why foul Phèdre dies,
That she can't look into her husband's eyes.
Your death Hippolytus will thus proclaim
Confirms his story and confirms your blame.
How could I answer your accuser? I
Would be outdone no matter what I try.
Then he would revel in his triumph here
And slander you to all who lend an ear.
Oh let a bolt of lightning strike me! Yet
Be truthful to me. Can you not forget

---

[37] With her other psychological defense mechanisms failing, she turns to fanatasy. In her case it is the ultimate fantasy of death which she believes will end and thus solve all her own problems.
[38] Their ancestor Minos is descended from Jupiter.

Him? How does he appear to your eyes now?

Phèdre

I see him as a monster. That is how.

Oenone

Then why give all the victory away?
Dare blame him first of crimes that he today
Can charge are yours. Who could disprove it? Soon
The world will harshly blame him. You've the boon
As well that in his haste he left his sword!
Your mental state of course is in accord
Along with warnings to his father and
His prior exile done at your command.

Phèdre

How could I slander, crush the guiltless? How?

Oenone

I only ask you keep your silence now.
I also tremble and feel your remorse.
I'd rather face a thousand deaths of course.
But since you're lost without this remedy,
Preserving you now matters most to me.
I'll do the talking and when I am done
The angered King will just exile his son.
A father's still a father. Therefore, he

54

Will always choose the lighter penalty--
But if somebody's blood must now be shed,
Of course it's better it be his instead.
Your honor is too dear to wager it.
Whatever conscience says, you must submit.
To save your battered honor, Madame, you
Must sacrifice it all, your virtue, too.
I see the King.

Phèdre

Hippolytus as well!
My awful end! His rude eyes bode me ill!
You've my permission. I give in to you.
I cannot help myself in what I do!

Scene 4

(Theseus, Hippolytus, Phèdre, Oenone, Theramenes)

Theseus

The fates have finally ceased opposing us
And gave me back to you....

Phèdre

Stop, Theseus.
Do not profane the charming sight I see.
I don't deserve the things you say to me.
You've been offended. Jealous Fortune did

55

Not spare your wife when you were not amid
Us here. Unfit to please or see you, I
Just think of hiding far beyond your eye.[39]

Scene 5

(Theseus, Hippolytus, Theramenes)

Theseus

Why did she greet me that peculiar way,
My son?

Hippolytus

       For reasons she alone can say.
Please, Father, grant my wish. I now implore
You never let me see her any more.
Just grant your trembling son the right to flee
From every place that she might ever be.

Theseus

You'd leave me, Son?

Hippolytus

It never was my thought

---

[39] In case there was any ever doubt, Phèdre of course demonstrates here that one can lie with the truth.

56

To have her here. You were the one who brought
Her here then left requiring Phèdre and
Aricia to live in Trozene land,
Obliging me to be the guardian for
Them both. I need not do that any more.
I've spent enough of my youth in the wood
*To prove to the unskilled my gifts are good.
Can I not quit such idleness to stain
My spear with nobler, better blood? Unchain
Me! Even at a younger age, Sir, you
Had shown those tyrants and those monsters, too,
The weight of your strong arm. You had as well
Assured no insolence could safely dwell
Along the coasts of either of our seas[40].
You freed the traveler from such fears as these.
Once Hercules had heard the stories, too,
He stopped and took a rest because of you.
Although you're great, nobody knows my name.
I cannot even match my mother's fame.
Please let me test my courage. Let me try
To slay some monsters that you missed. Then I
Can lay the spoils of honor at your feet
Or leave a lasting memory of the feat
And of my days and deeds so nobly done
That prove to all the world I was your son.

Theseus

What is this wide-spread horror that I see

---

[40] Again, the Ionian and Aegean Seas.

57

That makes my desperate family run from me?
Oh gods, if my return has brought such fear
Why was I pulled from prison to be here?
I only had one friend[41] who amorous
Desired the wife of one from Epirus.
I'm sad to say I tried to help him find
Her. Irritated, Fate then made us blind.
I was unarmed. The husband ambushed me.
And then, through many tears, I had to see
My friend thrown to those awful monsters who
Then feasted on his blood. I suffered, too.
The brute shut me in somber caverns well
Beneath the ground close to the bounds of Hell.
The gods heard me when six long months had passed.
In time, I learned to trick my guards at last.
I purged the world of that base enemy.
I made him fodder for the monsters he
Kept. Joyous, next I thought of coming here
To be with everything I hold most dear--
Yet, all the welcome I receive is fright,
No hugs, just people running out of sight.
Why, meeting all the terror I provoke
I'm better in the pit of which I spoke.
Now Phèdre says I've been offended. Who
Did such a deed? And why no vengeance? Do
Those Greeks who made such use of my strong arm
Now shelter such a criminal from harm?
You give no answer. You, my very son,
Could you have joined in any evil done?

---

[41] Again, this is Pirithoüs as noted above.

Let's go inside. I've kept these doubts too long.
I'll know at once this felony, this wrong.
In Phèdre's state she'll tell me truthfully.

Scene 6

(Hippolytus, Theramenes)

Hippolytus

What did he mean by that? It frightens me.
Will Phèdre, still the prey of her extreme
Behavior, now admit her awful scheme?
Oh, gods! What would he say?! What awful dose
Of poison love has spread! Our home's morose!
I'm frightened by such black forebodings though
The guiltless shouldn't fear. It's time we go
Attempt by happy speech to move him to
Be kind to me as love would have him do
And tell him of my love. Though he may try
To test it harshly, it will never die.

ACT IV

Scene 1

(Theseus, Oenone)

Theseus

What do I hear?! A fool and traitor, he
Would so disgrace his father's dignity?!
Oh, Destiny, you would pursue me so,
I don't know where I am or where I go!
My tenderness and kindness were for naught!
Audacious scheme! Abject and horrid thought!
To have his black love, keep his awful course
His arrogance would even turn to force!
I recognize the sword he planned to use--
My noble gift that he now would abuse!
His many blood ties were no stop for him--
Yet Phèdre's silence in the interim--
Was it some hope to spare the guilty man?

Oenone

To spare instead the father was her plan.
A crazy lover's scheme crushed her with shame.
She saw the awful crime in his eyes. Blame
Her not. Phèdre was slowing dying and
She planned to take her life by her own hand.
I saw her raise her arm. I rushed fast to
Stop her and thereby saved her life for you.

With so much pity for her cares and fears,
I understood (against my will) her tears.[42]

Theseus

The traitor could not help but blanche then! He
Quite clearly winced with fear when he met me.[43]
He shocked me by his lack of cheerfulness.[44]
His cold embrace then chilled my tenderness.
This guilty love which eats him up, had he
Declared it back in Athens, too? Tell me.

Oenone

Sir, please remember how your Queen protested
And how she hated what he had suggested.

Theseus

And so it started back in Trozene? Where?

Oenone

I've told you all that happened. Sir, I fear
I've left the Queen too long in all her grief.
Please let me go and offer my relief.

---

[42] Since Oenone is using another's tears as proof of the thing they
allegedly say, perhaps we could call Oenone's statements "tearsay".
[43] "Tearsay" is now supported by "fearsay."
[44] Now we introduce "Cheersay."

Scene 2

(Theseus, Hippolytus)

Theseus

Ah! There he is! Such noble bearing! He
Must fool the world as well as he fooled me.
How can a foul adulterer appear
The sparkling model of true virtue? There
Should be some outer signs or marks so one
Could still divine such sin inside a son![45]

Hippolytus

May I inquire what fatal, awful cloud
Has darken up a face so nobly browed?
Would you not dare confide the thing to me?

Theseus

You traitor! Dare you come where I could see
You? Monster heaven's lightning bolts have missed!
I slew all other thieves. Just you persist!
And even after taking your foul lust
Up to your father's bed, you find you must
Display the head of such an enemy!

---

[45] However, Theseus has already judged his son on the basis of tears, fear and other outward marks. Jealousy of course is not founded on logic.

You show up here in all your infamy
Instead of searching out some foreign place
Where people neither know my name or face--
Flee, traitor, never come back here to test
The anger I can barely now arrest!
I'll have enough disgrace in what I've done,
In giving life to such a horrid son.
I hardly need to stain my great deeds by
The shame of causing my own son to die.
Be gone! And if you are not smitten fast
And added to the list of felons past
I've punished, you'll take care you never set
Another rash step in this country. Get
Out, I say, and quickly do it so
My kingdom's purged of evil. Leave us! Go!
And you, Neptune, back when my courage rid
Your shores of awful killers, what you did
In payment, you'll recall, was make the vow
To grant my first request[46]. And until now
I've held off asking. Even captive I
Did not invoke your awful powers. By
So doing I have saved them and therefore
Can use them now when I now need them more.
Avenge a grieving father I beg you!
I throw this traitor to your anger to
Let loose his blood to choke his awful lust
And I shall find your furious actions just!

---

[46] Theseus refers to his clearing bandits from the route to Athens.
According legend, Neptune built the walls around the city.

Hippolytus

What?! Phèdre said I'm guilty of a crime!
Such awful horror mutes my soul. Sir, I'm
So caught off guard by this foul blow that I
Now cannot speak however hard I try.

Theseus

It was your hope, you traitor, that her fear
Would keep her still and shroud your foul deeds here.
You should have never left your sword. For it
Condemns you though her silence might acquit--
Perhaps you should have crowned your evil by
A single muting blow to make her die!

Hippolytus

I'm rightly angered at a lie so black,
And should use truth to counter the attack,
But I suppress a secret close to you.
At least show me respect in what I do.
Don't make your troubles worse. Judge me instead
By who I am and by the life I've led.
Small crimes always proceed the great ones since
We must exceed some smaller bounds before
We're ready for the ones most vicious. We
Both know that crime, like virtue, has degree.
You never see pure shyness leap into
The foul licentiousness you'd have me do.
A single day can't change the virtuous

64

Into the murderous or incestuous.
Nursed at the breast of a chaste heroine,
I've not forgotten where my roots begin.
Then Pittheus[47] who's praised in all the lands
Deigned to instruct me when I'd left her hands.
I don't desire to paint myself too well.
But if some share of virtue from them fell
To me, I think I've shown my hatred, too,
For just those evils they dare say I do.
That's how Greece knows Hippolytus. They see
I push my virtue till it's harsh in me.
They all know my austerity won't sway.
They know my heart is pure as light of day.
How could you think such slander of me true?

Theseus

Yes, that's the very pride condemning you!
I see the main cause of your coldness now.
Just Phèdre charms your lewd eyes. You allow
No love that's innocent. Instead you are
Indifferent to all others near and far.

Hippolytus

No, father, it's too much to hide from you.
My heart has not refused to love. I do
Confess here at your feet of love I've had

---

[47] King of Trozene and grandfather of Theseus who raised both Theseus
and Hippolytus.

And still have, Sir, despite what you forbade.
Aricia holds me captive. She has won.
Pallas's daughter conquered your own son,
And I adoring her must break your law.
I think of her with every breath I draw.

Theseus

You love her? Heavens! No, the trick is plain.
You cover up worse crimes by crimes you feign.[48]

Hippolytus

I've stayed away for six months. Still I love
Her and I came in fear to tell you of
My passion. What? Will nothing make you see
You're wrong? What frightful oath's required of me?
May earth and heaven, all of nature, too....

Theseus

Such perjury is what you scoundrels do.
Spare me your irritating words if they
Are all your bogus virtue has to say.

Hippolytus

Although my virtue may seem false to you,

---

[48] Does this make sense? Presumably Theseus is treating the love of
Phèdre as a malum in se while the love of Aricia is only a malum
prohibitum which Theseus has the power to rectify.

Your Phèdre's heart knows what I say is true.

Theseus

Your awful impudence is angering me!

Hippolytus

How long and where then shall my exile be?

Theseus

If you were past Alcides' columns[49], it
Would be too close for me to find it fit.

Hippolytus

Charged with the frightening crime that you suspect,
Who'll pity such a son that you reject?

Theseus

Go find some friends who honor incest, who
Applaud adultery as much as you,
Some ingrates and some traitors who rebel
Against the law and dignity as well.

---

[49] I.e., Hercules' columns at the straights of Gibraltar which then marked
the limits of the known world.

67

Hippolytus

You speak of incest and adultery
Though I say nothing. Yet, your Phèdre, she
Is from a lineage and a mother who
Did horrors worse than any I could do.[50]

Theseus

What? Your black rage is uncontrolled now? I'm
Demanding that you leave here one last time.
Leave traitor! Do not wait and force me to
Have you dragged off as I shall shortly do!

Scene 3

(Theseus)

Theseus

You wretch, you run to meet a certain doom.
For Neptune by that river of the tomb
Once gave his word to me and he will do
Just as he said. A vengeful god hunts you.
You won't escape. Yet, I loved you and I'm
Still troubled though I know your awful crime.
But you have forced this condemnation. For

---

[50] He apparently alludes to the fact that Phèdre's mother had an affair with a bull.

Have any sons offended fathers more?
Oh gods, who see such sadness plaguing me,
How could I have a son as sick as he?

Scene 4

(Phèdre, Theseus)

Phèdre

I've come to you, Sir, full of proper fear.
Your voice is strong enough for me to hear.
I tremble that your will will soon be done.
If it is not too late, please save your son.
Please spare your flesh and blood and equally
The horrors that his pains would bring to me.
I was the cause of what you now would do.
Don't make me suffer knowing that is true.

Theseus

My hand is free of my own blood. Yet he,
The foul ingrate, has not escaped from me.
His doom is in the hands of a Great One.
Neptune owes me. You'll see our vengeance done.

Phèdre

What?! Angry wishes, Neptune in your debt....

Theseus

Are you afraid he hasn't heard me yet?
Then add your sincere prayers to mine as well.
What are the dark facts of the crime? Please tell
Me. Fire my anger. It has been too slow.
And yet his crimes are worse than you could know.
He slanders you in anger and he tries
To make me think your mouth is full of lies.
To Aricia he maintains he pledged
His heart.

Pheadra

What? Sir?!

Theseus

Or so he has alleged
To me. But I reject it as a trick.
Let's hope that Neptune's justice will be quick.
I'll go before his altar once more now
And press him to uphold his timeless vow.

Scene 5

(Phèdre)

Phèdre

He's gone. What information have I here?
What awful fire revives in my heart? Hear
The burst of thunder, gods! Such news! I came
To help his son. It was my only aim.
I ripped myself away from Oenone
And gave in to the sadness plaguing me.
Who knows how far repentance could have gone?
Perhaps I could have placed all blame upon
Myself. Cut short, perhaps I was about
To speak the frightful truth, to let it out.
Hippolytus can feel--but not for me!
Aricia has his heart and only she!
When I told him my feelings he was so
Ungrateful, cold and proud I thought that no
Love ever moves a heart he keeps so closed--
To every woman he must be opposed.
And yet another woman cracked his pride
And found some mercy there. Might one decide
Instead his heart is moved quite easily,
He tolerates the world except for me.?
Why should I then have thought of his defense?

Scene 6

(Pheadra, Oenone)

Pheadra

You want to hear the latest incidence?

Oenone

No, but to tell the truth I come afraid.
I pale in fear of plans you may have made.
I worry that your rage is killing you.

Phèdre

I had a rival. Could you think it true?

Oenone

What?

Phèdre

He's in love now. I can have no doubt.
Untamable by all, he went about
Offended by respect, ignoring pleas,
Yet now submits to Aricia. She's
Now somehow found the way into his heart.

What? Aricia?

Phèdre

Still more misery!
What new torments could be reserved for me?!
I've suffered so. Yet ecstasies and fears,
The fury of my love, the horror of my tears,
His mean refusal and its injury
All pale beside what's now tormenting me!
They are in love! What charms hid the affair?
How would they meet? How long together? Where?
You knew! Why let me be the victim of
Their tricks? You should have told me of their love.[51]
How often were they known to meet, to talk,
Or step into for the forest for a walk?
They freely gazed in one another's eyes
While Heaven blessed their innocence and sighs.
Remorseless they could have the love they see
And bask in every day's serenity
While I was outcast from cruel nature's sight
And forced to hide by day and flee the light.
My hopes could only be in death. So I
Just waited for the moment I would die.
My food was gall, my drink the sobs I held.
I was too closely watched. Though sorrow welled

---

[51] As a self-defense mechanism, she thus turns to projection: she projects the blame on Oenone.

I dared not find a remedy in tears.
They'd find me out. All chained up in my fears
I was an inmate who was forced to keep
A stoic face. I could not even weep![52]

Oenone

They'll meet no more. What are the profits of
Their passion?

Phèdre

They will always be in love!
Why, even as I speak (oh, horrid thought!),
They brave the ills a lover's wrath has wrought.
Despite this exile which would part them, they
Will make a thousand oaths that they will stay
Together. I can't stand their happiness.
Have pity for my jealousy, distress.
Aricia must be crushed. My husband's hate
For all her clan we shall rejuvenate.
She can't be punished lightly here when I'm
Convinced her evils dwarf her brothers' crime.
I'll beg him jealously till I'm obeyed.
What am I doing? Has my reason strayed?
I'm jealous yet it's Theseus I implore!
My husband lives and I love still. Yet for
Which one? I claim which heart? Each word I've said

---

[52] Yet, she speaks honestly in these fourteen lines, giving a chilling summary of the toll and efforts of well-closeted love.

Has made the hair stand upright on my head.
My crimes have gone beyond all boundaries.
Deceit and incest--I've joined both of these.
My murderous hands are quick to vengeance. They
Would spill some guiltless blood here right away.
I'm miserable! I live? I stand and see
The sacred Sun who shares its race with me?[53]
The parents of the gods[54] were my kin. My
Family fills the universe, the sky.
Where can I hide? Run to the night! That's where.
But no--my father guards the dark urn there.[55]
In his severe hands Minos holds, they say,
The fate of phantoms death has sent his way.
Oh, how his shade would tremble in surprise
In seeing his own girl before his eyes
Forced to admit her many crimes which well
Might number some not even known in Hell!
What would my father say to such a sight?
I think I'd see him drop the urn. He might
Then choose some novel punishment. I'm vexed.
I fear he'd execute his daughter next.
Forgive me.[56] Some cruel god has torn apart
Your family. See the vengeance in my heart.
I never had a sample of its fruits,

---

[53] Again, Phèdre's mother was the daughter of Helios.
[54] Phèdre can make this claim because Helios was the son of Hyperion (brother of Kronos and the Titans). Hyperion was in turn the son of Uranus (the Sky) and Gaia (the Earth).
[55] Minos became a judge in Hades after Daedalus caused him to be scalded to death in a bath.
[56] Is she hallucinating? Does she actually see her father now?

But ever have the shame the crime imputes!
Misfortune hounds me to my final breath.
Tormented, I surrender now to death.

Oenone

Ah, Madame, don't fall prey to foolish fear.
The error could be seen as natural here.
You love. You can't defeat your destiny.
A fatal charm dragged you unwillingly.
Is such a thing unknown to everyone?
Is yours the only battle Love has won?
Such frailty's normal in all humankind.
You're mortal. Bear the fate of all your kind.
You're angry at a yoke tied long ago.
Why, even gods, Olympians sounding so
Horrific in condemning what we do,
Have sometimes had forbidden passions, too.[57]

Phèdre

What do I hear? Advice? Temerity!
Still trying to the end to ruin me,
You wretch? You are the reason I'm undone.[58]

---

[57] Although Phèdre's response is violent, the philosophical issues
Oenone raises are of course profound ones. How can Phèdre be
responsible for an involuntary love? Furthermore, if the gods (who are
better than mortals) do similar things, how can such actions be wrong?
To claim otherwise is to claim the gods do wrong and would this not be
blasphemy?

[58] Here Phèdre slips again into projection as an ego defense.

You stopped me dying when I had begun.
Your prayers made me forget my duty and
Talk to Hippolytus though I had planned
To shun him. Who put you in charge? How can
You dare accuse or slander such a man?
Perhaps you've caused his death! A father's plea,
A sacrilege, might soon be granted! Flee,
You awful monster! I will hear no more.
Leave me alone to face fates I deplore.
May heaven pay its debt in full to you!
Your punishment--may it give terror to
All others who with awful verbal skill
Would work a lover's weaknesses until
He slides that slippery slope to which his heart
Inclines and thereby fouls himself. Depart!
The flatterer is surely the worst thing
That Heaven's wrath could ever give a king!

Oenone
(Alone)

Oh, gods! I gave up all as I have served.
And what is my reward? It's well deserved.

77

ACT V

Scene 1

(Hippolytus, Aricia)

Aricia

How can you hold your tongue with such a threat?
You dearly love your King and father yet
You'd leave him so mistaken? Cruelty!
You could forsake me weeping as you see?
Then go and separate yourself from me.
But save your life at least when going. Be
Forceful and defend your honor so
Your father's prayer's withdrawn before you go.
There still is time. What foolishness makes you
Make things as easy for her as you do?
Tell Theseus the truth!

Hippolytus

          What could be said?
Should I have told him of his shameful bed?
Should I have spoken plainly of disgrace
And watched the red shame spread across his face?
You are the only one who knows what's true.
I only shared my heart with gods and you.
Do not forget my words were given sealed.
If possible, forget what I revealed
And never let a mouth so pure give air

To any aspect of this foul affair.
Instead confide in justice from on high.
The gods will be concerned, will justify
Me. Phèdre will be punished at the time
The gods consider fitting for her crime.
She won't escape. That's all I ask of you.
I'll let my anger have free license to
Address the rest. Escape your slavery!
Dare break your bonds and run away with me!
Run from a foul and filthy kingdom where
All goodness must breathe in such poisoned air!
You now can profit from the chaos my
Disgrace has brought and leave unnoticed. I
Can guarantee to you the means to flee.
I've been your guardian till now. And we
Have strong men who will side with us instead--
For Sparta calls and Argos' arms are spread.
They are our common friends. They'll hear our call.
We can't let Phèdre profit from our fall
And drive us both from our paternal throne
To give her son a crown that's ours alone.
The moment's right and we must seize it. Yet,
You seem unsure, afraid and still upset.
It's for your sake alone I am so bold.
When I am hot, how could you be so cold?
Because I'm banished? I don't understand.

Aricia

What do you mean? Such exile would be grand
Allowing me to link my destiny

79

With yours and let the rest forget of me!
But as we are not married how could we
Now steal away together honorably?
I know that right and honor don't command
Me to remain chained by father, and
Such flight would not be from *my* parents. Too,
I'd run from tyrants as the virtuous do--
Yet, you love me--my honor I'm afraid....

Hippolytus

I care too much and never would degrade
You. No, a nobler plan I'm offering you:
Your freedom with me as your husband, too.
Freed from misfortune, heaven would permit
Our bond despite what others think of it.
True marriage isn't always formal.[59] There
Remains in Trozene (mid the old tombs where
My family's princes have been laid to rest)
A temple liars fear, a temple blessed,
A place of no false oaths. No one would dare
Speak falsehood there. All lies are punished there,
And there we can, if you believe in me,
Confirm our endless bond most solemnly.
The god one worships there will witness. We
Will pray to him together that he be
As father to us both. I will appeal
To chaste Diana, then to Juno. She'll

---

[59] Theseus's marriage demonstrates the converse: formal marriage is not
always true.

Join with the other gods who all can see
My tenderness and gladly vouch for me.

Aricia

The King is coming. Quickly run away.
To hide my plans to go I'll briefly stay--
Go on but leave me with a faithful guide
To lead my timid steps back to your side.

Scene 2

(Theseus, Aricia, Ismene)

Theseus

Oh gods, make plain my troubles, make them clear
And share with me the truth I'm seeking here.

Aricia

Ismene, go and ready us a boat.

Scene 3

(Theseus, Aricia)

Theseus

Your color's changed. You're quiet I now note.
Hippolytus was here. I ask you why.

Aricia

He left for good. He came to say good-bye.

Theseus

Your eyes knew how to tame him, and you can
Now claim you caused the first love in the man.

Aricia

I can't deny the truth of this. The son
Inherited no hatred from you, none.
He doesn't treat me as a felon or....

Theseus

I understand. Eternal love he swore.
But don't rely on what he said to you.
He's said as much to other women, too.

Aricia

He has?

Theseus

You should have stopped the fickle man
Who'd make you nothing but his courtesan.

Aricia

Can you believe those awful things you say
About a son who lives a noble way?
How can you know so little of his heart?
Can you not tell the good and bad apart?
Does some horrendous cloud obscure the view
Of goodness that all others see but you?
You can't surrender him to slander.   Please,
Stop yourself. Revoke your murderous pleas.
Though angry heaven takes our victims, we
May often find that gift a penalty.

Theseus

You try in vain to hide his crimes from me.
You're blinded by your love and cannot see
The ingrate as he is. My proof instead
Is sure, and I have seen the tears she shed.

Aricia

Be careful, Sir. Your hands have freed mankind
From awful monsters of most every kind--
And yet not all were slain.   At least not one--
I can't go on. I've orders from your son.
I know the highest reverence he has for
You. I would mortify him saying more.
I imitate his modesty and go
Before I'm forced to say more than I do.

Scene 4

(Theseus)

Theseus

What does she think? What does she really say
Between the lines in such a broken way?
They use some vain pretense to addle me?
Or torture me with some conspiracy?
Although I know I'm right to be severe,
I have some pleas from my own heart I hear.
Some secret pity shocks and bothers me.
I need to talk some more with Oenone.
It's time I clarify things for myself.
Guards! Have Oenone come here by herself.

Scene 5

(Theseus, Panope)

Panope

I don't know what the Queen has on her mind.
She's upset and I fear what we could find.
Her face is tinted over in despair
With deathly white already painted there.
Chased off in shame, already Oenone
Has jumped into the bowels of the sea.
How could she do it? No one here knows why,
And now the waves obscure where she must lie.

Theseus

What?

Panope

Phèdre's suffering though Oenone's dead.
The troubles multiply within her head.
Sometimes to ease her secret pains and fears
She grabs her children, bathes them with her tears.
And then maternal love stops suddenly.
She pushes them away in horror. She
Then walks about at random while her eyes
Are fixed on faces she can't recognize.
She tried to write three times but changed her mind
And tore the letters up. Sir, please be kind.

Consent to see and help her in reply.

Oenone's dead and Phèdre wants to die?!
Bring back my son! I must defend him! We
Must talk and I will listen carefully.
Do not be quick to grant my wrong request,
Neptune! Refusing it would now be best!
My witnesses--perhaps they lied to me
And I appealed to you too hastily--
Oh what despair might follow what I've done!

Scene 6

(Theseus, Theramenes)

Theseus

Is that you Theramenes? Where's my son?
When he was young I charged you with his care.
But why the tears that I see flowing there?
How is my son?

                    Theramenes
                    It now is too late for
Such cares. Hippolytus exists no more.

Theseus

Oh gods!

Theramenes

I saw the best of mortals fall,
And I dare say the purest of them all.

Theseus

My son's no more? When I would give my arm
To him, the gods are quick to do him harm?
What blow has stricken him? What thunder blast?

Theramenes

Through Trozene's outer gates we just had passed.
He rode his chariot. His guards were sad.
In silence, too, they circled round the lad.
Pensive, he took the Mycenaean[60] road.
He barely held the reins taut as he rode,
And his great horses that we used to see
Obey their master's voice so eagerly
Now walked downcast. They seemed to imitate
A master's sadness in their mournful gait.
From deep beneath the waves a frightful cry

---

[60] Mycenae, a bronze age center, was an ancient Greek city located on the Northeastern part of the Peloponnessus.

Disturbed the peaceful airs that filled the sky.
A fearsome voice then deep beneath the ground
Groaned in response to that first awful sound.
Deep down within our hearts our blood froze and
We saw the manes on all the horses stand
Up straight. The watery plain then arched its back
Into a foaming mountain. The attack
Was on: the waves spewed out and we could see
An awful monster rising from the sea.
His face was huge and armed with horns. The grim
Beast had foul yellow scales all over him.
Untamable, that beast, that dragon next
Heaved up and coiled its awful parts. It flexed
As endless bellows caused the shores to quake.
The sky was horrified to see it snake
And move the earth as it fouled, too, the air.
In fear, the waves that brought it drew back. There
Then followed flight--no point in being brave--
All sought some shelter that some temple gave--
Except Hippolytus. The hero's son
Just stopped his horses, grabbed his spears, hurled one
With his sure hand right at the monster. He
Then hit and wounded it most grievously.
The monster bounding in fierce rage and pain
Fell roaring at the horses' feet. Again,
It rolled. It bared a burning mouth that spoke
With blood and fire. All covered up in smoke,
The frightened horses had forgotten all.
They didn't know their reins or master's call.
He tried in vain to take control. They bled.
They gnashed their bits. Their mouths were foamy red.

Next in this horrid spectacle some say
A god was seen, too, spurring them away.
In fear they dashed across the rocks from us.
The axles screamed and broke. Hippolytus
Then saw his chariot flying, crashing. He
Fell tangled in the reins most pitifully.
Oh, what a horrid scene! I am afraid
I'll cry forever at the sight he made.
Dragged by the very horses he had fed,
I saw your brave son struggle as they fled.
He tried to call them back. That scared them more.
They ran. His body was one wound, one sore.
Our sad cries echoed all around the plain.
At last their stamina began to wane.
They stopped close by the ancient tombs that hold
His family's relics, bones that now lie cold.
I ran there sighing. His guards followed me
Upon a trail of blood there off the sea--
The rocks were painted crimson where he bled.
There thorns held red locks ripped out of his head.
When I arrived, I called him, offered my
Hand. He just cracked then quickly closed one eye.
"The gods have killed a guiltless man," he said.
"Look after Aricia when I'm dead.
My friend, if Father learns the truth one day
And pities how they treated me you may
Appease my blood and ghost if you will tell
Our Theseus to treat his captive well,
To give her...." At that word the hero died.
I held his tattered body by my side,
The work of angry gods, his sad corpse you

Would never recognize as one you knew.

Theseus

My son! My dearest hope! I erred! You fell!
Inexorable gods, you served me much too well!
I'm cursed with everlasting grief and blame!

Theramenes

And then, Sir, timid Aricia came.
She would by flight escape your anger, and
The two would wed before the gods. As planned,
She walked up. Then she saw the bloody grass
And smoke and saw (and, what a sight, alas!)
Hippolytus all white and formless. She
Would not at first believe the tragedy.
Not recognizing her Hippolytus
She tried to find his whereabouts from us.
When finally satisfied that he had died,
She glanced accusingly at Heaven, cried,
And trembling, almost lifeless with despair,
She fainted, falling by her lover there.
Ismene was nearby and brought relief:
She called her back to life or rather grief.
I come in wake of matters I detest
To tell you of a hero's last request
And thus acquit an obligation to
A dying friend. In doing what I do,
I look upon his mortal enemy!

(Theseus, Phèdre, Theramenes, Panope, Guards)

Theseus

My son's dead. You have triumphed thoroughly.
What should I fear? My heart forgives him for
Suspicions reason might dwell on some more.
But, Phèdre, he is dead. Accept your win.
Though right or wrong, your revels may begin.
I'll let my eyes be fooled forever. You
Accused him. I'll believe your words were true.
His death provides sufficient grief for me
Without the need of searching on to see
What other evils lurk. They could not bring
Him back; they might just trouble more the King.
Quite far away from you and here, I shall
Escape that bloody image of it all.
His memory, my confusion are my curse.
I am condemned throughout the universe
That rises up as one to punish me.
My fame exacerbates my penalty--
Less known, I might go hide more easily.
Despising even honors gods do me,
I'll go and mourn their awful favors where
I cannot tire them with more worthless prayer.
If they still have some bounty left in store
For me, it won't replace my loss before.

Phèdre

No, Theseus, my silence is unjust.
I have to break it with the truth. I must
Defend his innocence.

Theseus

                    Oh, father's woe!
It was your word that had him punished so!
Cruel witch! Could you still make excuses? How....

Phèdre

Please hear me, Theseus. Time's precious now.
Your son was chaste. Instead, Sir, it was I
Who dared look out with incest in my eye.
The heavens put that fire within my breast.
Then awful Oenone did all the rest.
She knew your son rejected me. Her fear
Was he would make it all too public here.
Abusing my great weakness, wrongly, too,
She hastened to accuse him first to you.
She's punished now. To skirt my anger, she
Sought out a lighter death and drowned at sea.
I would have stabbed myself already would
That not have left his virtue stained. I could
Not. Thus, I chose a slower path to Hell
To give me time to tell what I must tell.
I've filled my veins with poisons from a jar
Medea brought to Athens once. They are

At work now, moving almost to my heart.
I feel an unknown chill begin to start.
I seem to see already through a mist
A sky and husband outraged I exist.
Death takes light from my eyes. The day regains
The purity I darkened with these stains.

Panope

She's dying, Sir!

Theseus

If only her foul crime
Could share her dark grave with her for all time!
Alas, my awful errors I now know.
Let's mix our tears with blood and let us go
Embrace what's left of our dear son. While there
We'll expiate a King's horrific prayer.
We'll pay my son the honor he is due.
To calm his irritated ghost we, too,
Shall take Aricia as our daughter. We
Shall pardon her her family's treachery.

The end